D1283455

Folk Medicine

North American Folklore

Children's Folklore
Christmas and Santa Claus Folklore
Contemporary Folklore
Ethnic Folklore
Family Folklore
Firefighters' Folklore
Folk Arts and Crafts
Folk Customs
Folk Dance
Folk Fashion
Folk Festivals
Folk Games
Folk Medicine
Folk Music
Folk Proverbs and Riddles
Folk Religion
Folk Songs
Folk Speech
Folk Tales and Legends
Food Folklore
Regional Folklore

North American Folklore

Folk Medicine

BY PETER SIELING

Mason Crest Publishers

Mason Crest Publishers Inc.
370 Reed Road
Broomall, Pennsylvania 19008
(866) MCP-BOOK (toll free)
www.masoncrest.com

First printing
1 2 3 4 5 6 7 8 9 10
Library of Congress Cataloging-in-Publication Data on file at the Library of Congress.
ISBN 1-59084-341-X
        1-59084-328-2 (series)

Design by Lori Holland.
Composition by Bytheway Publishing Services, Binghamton, New York.
Cover design by Joe Gilmore.
Printed and bound in the Hashemite Kingdom of Jordan.

Picture credits:
Corbis: pp. 6, 8, 12, 14, 15, 16, 18, 28, 30, 32, 38, 40, 48, 50, 64, 72, 80, 82, 84, 85, 86, 87, 88, 90, 96, 99
PhotoDisc: p. 74
Cover: "Grandma's Remedy" by Norman Rockwell © 1936 SEPS: Licensed by Curtis Publishing, Indianapolis, IN. www.curtispublishing.com

Printed by permission of the Norman Rockwell Family
© the Norman Rockwell Family Entities

Contents

Folklore grows from long-ago
seeds. Just as an acorn sends
down roots even as it shoots up
leaves across the sky, folklore is
rooted deeply in the past and
yet still lives and grows today.
It spreads through our modern
world with branches as wide
and sturdy as any oak's;
it grounds us in yesterday even
as it helps us make sense of
both the present and the future.

Introduction

by Dr. Alan Jabbour

W HAT DO A TALE, a joke, a fiddle tune, a quilt, a jig, a game of jacks, a saint's day procession, a snake fence, and a Halloween costume have in common? Not much, at first glance, but all these forms of human creativity are part of a zone of our cultural life and experience that we sometimes call "folklore."

The word "folklore" means the cultural traditions that are learned and passed along by ordinary people as part of the fabric of their lives and culture. Folklore may be passed along in verbal form, like the urban legend that we hear about from friends who assure us that it really happened to a friend of their cousin. Or it may be tunes or dance steps we pick up on the block, or ways of shaping things to use or admire out of materials readily available to us, like that quilt our aunt made. Often we acquire folklore without even fully realizing where or how we learned it.

Though we might imagine that the word "folklore" refers to cultural traditions from far away or long ago, we actually use and enjoy folklore as part of our own daily lives. It is often ordinary, yet we often remember and prize it because it seems somehow very special. Folklore is culture we share with others in our communities, and we build our identities through the sharing. Our first shared identity is family identity, and family folklore such as shared meals or prayers or songs helps us develop a sense of belonging. But as we grow older we learn to belong to other groups as well. Our identities may be ethnic, religious, occupational, or regional—or all of these, since no one has only one cultural identity. But in every case, the identity is anchored and strengthened by a variety of cultural traditions in which we participate and

3

share with our neighbors. We feel the threads of connection with people we know, but the threads extend far beyond our own immediate communities. In a real sense, they connect us in one way or another to the world.

Folklore possesses features by which we distinguish ourselves from each other. A certain dance step may be African American, or a certain story urban, or a certain hymn Protestant, or a certain food preparation Cajun. Folklore can distinguish us, but at the same time it is one of the best ways we introduce ourselves to each other. We learn about new ethnic groups on the North American landscape by sampling their cuisine, and we enthusiastically adopt musical ideas from other communities. Stories, songs, and visual designs move from group to group, enriching all people in the process. Folklore thus is both a sign of identity, experienced as a special marker of our special groups, and at the same time a cultural coin that is well spent by sharing with others beyond our group boundaries.

Folklore is usually learned informally. Somebody, somewhere, taught us that jump rope rhyme we know, but we may have trouble remembering just where we got it, and it probably wasn't in a book that was assigned as homework. Our world has a domain of formal knowledge, but folklore is a domain of knowledge and culture that is learned by sharing and imitation rather than formal instruction. We can study it formally—that's what we are doing now!—but its natural arena is in the informal, person-to-person fabric of our lives.

Not all culture is folklore. Classical music, art sculpture, or great novels are forms of high art that may contain folklore but are not themselves folklore. Popular music or art may be built on folklore themes and traditions, but it addresses a much wider and more diverse audience than folk music or folk art. But even in the world of popular and mass culture, folklore keeps popping up around the margins. E-mail is not folklore—but an e-mail smile is. And college football is not folklore—but the wave we do at the stadium is.

This series of volumes explores the many faces of folklore throughout the North American continent. By illuminating the many aspects of folklore in our lives, we hope to help readers of the series to appreciate more fully the richness of the cultural fabric they either possess already or can easily encounter as they interact with their North American neighbors.

Honey and various herbs are common ingredients in folk medicines.

ONE

A Definition of
Folk Medicine
Honey, Tar, and an
Alternate Worldview

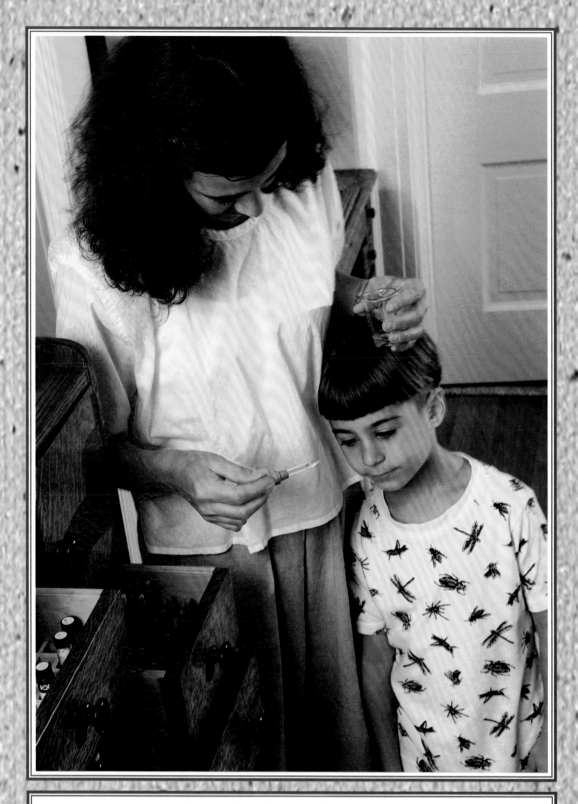

A mother doses her son with a home cure.

*I*MAGINE YOU wake up Monday morning remembering you forgot to study for a math test. You stayed up late last night to watch the end of that horror movie, and it gave you nightmares. After a short night of restless sleep, your head feels thick and your throat is itchy. You cough several dry, hacking coughs and moan weakly. "Mom, I feel sick," you croak.

"Here, darling, this will help." She brings in a bottle containing a black oily liquid and pours it into a spoon. It looks like the spoon is starting to dissolve, and you remember when she cooked up this stuff a couple months ago. With a shudder, you recall the recipe she used for this home remedy:

> *Put a tablespoonful of liquid tar into a shallow tin dish, and place it in boiling water until the tar is hot. To this add a pint of honey, and stir well for half an hour, adding to it a level teaspoonful of pulverized borax. Keep well corked in a bottle. Dose: Teaspoonful every one, two, or three hours, according to the severity of the cough.*

This highly effective cough remedy comes from a hundred-year-old pamphlet: *The Use of Honey in Cooking.* Here's how it works:

Mother aims the spoon toward your mouth. Suddenly your head clears and your throat doesn't feel that bad after all. You jump out of bed. "Hey, suddenly I feel like . . . great! I guess I don't need that medicine after all. Oops, I better get dressed. I just remembered I have a test in my favorite class today." Turns out, some things are worse than math tests.

Mother smiles. At last, a true miracle cure.

"FOLK medicine" has many meanings. For instance, it may mean modern "alternative medicine." Or it may mean an ancient form of healing that has been handed down from generation to generation. It may include a different perspective on reality from that found in traditional medical practice. In all likelihood, it may include some combination of all three definitions.

This newspaper clipping fell out of an old home-remedy medical book. It was clipped and saved by a local healer who no doubt saw many people die from a still-common sickness.

ONION POULTICE RECIPE AS CURE FOR PNEUMONIA

The News-Herald has been requested to publish this recipe for a pneumonia cure:

Take six to ten onions, chop fine, place over hot fire, mix with equal amount of rye meal and enough vinegar to form a thick paste. Stir thoroughly. Let simmer 5 to 10 minutes. Place paste in cotton bag, large enough to cover lungs, apply to chest as hot as patient can stand it. Before it gets cold, apply another, continuing to reheat the poultices. In a few hours the patient will be out of danger. Usually three or four applications are sufficient but continue until perspiration starts from the chest.

This simple remedy was concocted many years ago by one of the best physicians New England had, who never lost a patient with this disease. George L. Brown, of Littleton, Mass., has distributed hundreds of the copies of these recipes and it has been widely published. Mr. Brown says in his lifetime he has never known the cure to fail, even after the attending physician gave up all hope.

Barrenwort was thought to prevent pregnancy.

Walk into a modern pharmacy and you'll find shelves full of herbal remedies for everything from the common cold to herbal extracts to increase your intelligence. With overfilled doctor's offices, patients often feel like an **inanimate** part on an assembly line. They wait for an hour reading year-old parenting and health magazines, sitting between a doubtful-looking fellow with tuberculosis and a drippy smeary three-year-old who keeps wiping his nose on their armrest and coughing at them. When they are finally admitted to the examination room, they sit on an ice-cold steel table for another 30 minutes. The doctor rushes in with a clipboard and asks several perfunctory questions. The nurse takes their blood pressure and hands them a prescription scrawled with handwriting they can't decipher. Then they are directed to the receptionist, who magically produces a large bill.

Dissatisfaction with both the cost and quality of modern medicine creates a thriving alternative system. Before spending money on a doctor and his powerful chemicals, the patient may try less expensive herbal remedies. Pharmacies stock shelves of herbals: gingko biloba, ginseng, evening primrose oil, echinacea, feverfew. They are sold through a legal loophole as "nutritional supplements" rather than medicines (to the dismay of some traditional health-care professionals).

*Medieval crusaders carried St. John's Wort with them to
treat sore muscles. Today, many people take this plant as a
natural antidepressant.*

The practitioners of alternative medicine
likewise are forbidden by law to charge for
their services. These practitioners practice
"medicine without a license" and accept donations instead of a fee. Conventional medical
practitioners frequently frown on alternative
medicine, partly because of the danger of a false diagnosis and
improper treatment—and partly because of the competition to
conventional medicine.

Folk medicine may also refer to medicine as practiced by
primitive tribes in various countries, including shamans and
medicine men who perform rituals and dances to exorcise
demons. Included with these practices are a wide variety of
herbal remedies. For years, Western scientists scoffed at the
"voodoo witch doctor" stuff that showed up in pages of the *National Geographic* magazine. Then a closer examination showed
that many of the herbal potions really worked. Scientists traveled
into the deserts and rain forests to learn how the primitive medicine men and women practiced. They analyzed the chemical
components of medicinal plants to find and isolate the active
chemicals.

Folk medicine also sometimes refers to medicine as practiced
before the age of antibiotics. Diseases ran unchecked except by
quarantining victims. The doctor could be hours away by buggy,
and his methods may have been only a slight improvement over

the common people's remedies. Folks used what was on hand to assist the sick body to heal itself. We no longer apply mustard plasters or leeches; we don't mix up dried gizzard skins and sugar to cure stomachache— but families often still have their own favorite tried-and-true remedies.

Folk medicine differs from conventional medicine both in its cures and in its perception of sickness itself. Folk practitioners don't use prescription drugs. They can't prescribe them by law, but in addition, artificial chemicals are seen as unnatural and more dangerous. Meanwhile, conventional medical doctors tend

---

The body is an amazing thing and not fully understood, even by modern science. It can heal itself. (Imagine a self-repairing car!)

Many folk medicines are the result of coincidence. Someone goes to the local medicine man with a bad cough. The medicine man boils some cherry bark and prescribes one teaspoonful as needed. It works great on this patient. The next patient has a cough caused by a different illness. The cherry infusion doesn't work, so the healer tries a little tar. That works great on this person. The next patient, however, doesn't respond either to tar or cherry bark, so the healer mixes the two and adds a little chloroform. The patient's cough, which was about to go away anyway, goes away. Now the healer thinks to himself, *I have invented a super cough syrup. I'll just make it this way from now on.* But the next person doesn't respond to the medicine, so the healer adds alcohol.

In most of these cases, the cough will disappear as the body heals itself of its illness. The patient thanks the medicine man. The medicine man thanks the plants and chemicals. But the healing came from within the patient. Sickness in not a natural state for the human body. A doctor can prescribe boiled broccoli for a headache, and if the patient eats it long enough, the headache will go away.

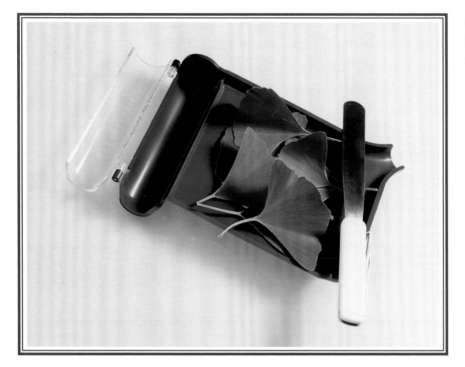

Gingko is a favorite natural remedy that is thought to improve the memory.

to neglect natural remedies altogether. Pharmaceutical companies spend their money developing synthetic chemical drugs because they can be patented and more profitable.

Folk practitioners tend to have a spiritual worldview. They believe in a God who is interested in the health of people. Many consider their healing ability a divine gift, and they believe God has provided the tools needed to heal. To the folk healer, an individual is a combination of body (the actual assembly of bones,

The traditional medicine of years past influences today's folk medicine.

The hips (fruit) of the dog rose are rich in Vitamin C. They can be crushed and mixed with honey to make a soothing treatment for sore throats. Mixed with vinegar, they can be used to treat headaches.

flesh, and organs), soul (the life force), and spirit (that immortal part that survives death). Modern doctors, on the other hand, whatever their personal religious convictions, are educated in a material worldview that assumes either that there is nothing beyond the physical world, or even if there is, that it is unmeasurable and irrelevant to science.

As technology progresses, conventional medicine of the current times is replaced by new discoveries. Today's conventional medicine becomes the folk medicine of the future. Folk medicine is in a state of constant change, quick to adopt new ideas but slow to drop old obsolete practices. In the year 2525, if man is still alive, human beings will look back at the medical practices of the 21st century and pity the poor folks who actually had to be cut open to be fixed, who had to suffer colds and the flu with nearly worthless quack remedies.

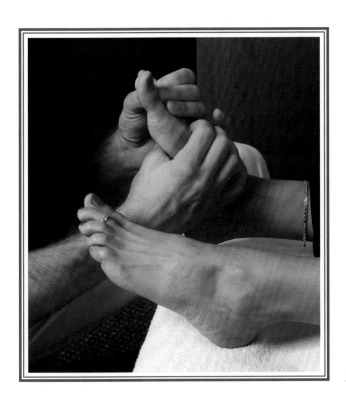

Massage is often a part of folk cures.

For centuries, medical practitioners have used a mortar and pestle for crushing natural substances into medicine.

TWO

Folk Medicine's
Common Roots
Ancient Medicine

The evening primrose is a mild sedative that is also good for asthma. Modern researchers are investigating whether this ancient remedy may help multiple sclerosis.

FOLK MEDICINE systems in their present form may be only a few hundred years old, but they have their origins in ancient systems. These strong systems adapted and accepted new information, such as the understanding that blood flows through arteries and veins, and the existence of microscopic germs. But many of folk medicine's basic practices and presuppositions can be traced to the beginning of recorded history.

We can learn about ancient civilizations' medical practices from the writings that have survived. The four major traditions in medicine go back about 4,000 years to Greece, Egypt, India, and China. Modern folk medicine is based on beliefs that can be traced through the earliest written languages.

ANCIENT EGYPTIAN MEDICINE

The reputation of ancient Egyptian physicians was unparalleled in the Middle East. The pharaohs sent their doctors to surrounding countries for consultation, treating the illnesses of the royal courts in neighboring kingdoms.

Archeologists have found fragments of **papyri** containing medical texts; two different texts have been discovered that are very different in tone and content. One seems to be a rational approach to diagnosing diseases, while the second is a random list of magic spells, potions, and cures for various afflictions. It doesn't describe diseases so most must be guessed at by the nature of the cures. To our eyes, the one appears to be a textbook containing a more systematic and clinical approach to healing. The other, with its magic formulas, seemed to be more of a folk reference.

The medicine chest of the Egyptian doctor contained a lot of meat products. Animal-based medicines were common and were sometimes intended to impart to the person characteristics of the animal. Often the purpose of the animal byproduct was simply to provide a vehicle for a less palatable medicine, such as mixing milk or honey with something else to improve or disguise the flavor. Other times meat itself was the drug of choice. The liver of

QUACK MEDICINE AMONG THE ANCIENT EGYPTIANS

Ancient Egyptians, like many modern North Americans, believed that thin hair makes a person look older and less confident. If you lived in Egypt 3,000 years ago, you might have tried this amazing formula for thicker, fuller, richer-looking hair. Results are guaranteed.

Mix in equal proportions the fat of:
lion
hippopotamus
crocodile
cat
snake
ibex
Anoint the bald head and rub vigorously.

Ancient Egyptians considered chamomile to be "consecrated to the sun." It can be used to make a soothing sedative tea; it was thought to prevent nightmares and promote sound sleep; it makes a gentle skin antiseptic; and it may help rheumatism.

various animals seems to be the most important medicinal meat. (Interestingly, liver has high concentrations of Vitamin A and B_{12}, vitamins that help promote health.)

Honey was one of the most commonly used ingredients in medicines. Like meat, it was used for its own virtues. (Today folk medicine still uses honey because of its antibiotic and antifungal properties.) Honey was the only sweet available to the Egyptians, so doctors used it to improve the palatability of other drugs.

Egyptian healers also used minerals called "natron," salts left after evaporation of water. The Egyptians used natron in mummification. Made into a paste, it was a medicine used for drawing water from inflammations and swelling.

Medicinal herbs were used extensively by the Egyptians, and some still have similar uses. One of those we can identify in the ancient texts is willow, which was used for treating swelling, inflammation, headache and toothache. Today we know that willow bark contains salicin, a compound now used to make aspirin, which not only treats headaches but is still one of the best drugs to treat inflammations and fevers.

Willow contains the same chemical compound as aspirin. It has been used for thousands of years to treat pain and fever.

Another medicinal plant used by the Egyptians was the pyrethrum daisy for head lice. Today scientists have synthesized pyrethrins based on the chemicals found in the daisies, and they are available as a pesticide.

Egyptian medicine made a distinction between natural and supernatural diseases. While there were many recipes for medicines, there were also numerous spells and incantations for curing the supernatural diseases. These are similar to modern folk practices in the backwaters of North America and the rest of the world.

ANCIENT GREEK MEDICINE

The ancient Greek language is still taught and Greek writings are well known and studied; Western Civilization traces its science and philosophy back through the Greek scientists and philosophers. Hippocrates, the Greek physician of the fifth century BC, wrote extensively on the practice of medicine.

The Greeks believed there were four elements in the universe: earth, air, fire, and water. Corresponding to these four elements were the four qualities: hot, cold, dry, and moist. All matter, including humans, contained more or less of the four elements and qualities.

According to Greek thought, the healthy human body is in a state of equilibrium or balance among four "humors" or fluids: blood, phlegm, yellow bile, and black bile. Each humor is a combination of two of the qualities. Illnesses were caused by imbalances in the humors. The aim of the physician was to oppose the cause of the disease, tipping the balance back toward the center. For example, a person with a fever should be cooled. Diseases related to overactivity required rest. Overeating required fasting.

Greek medicine further developed through the Roman physician Galen and spread throughout the **medieval** world. Today, folk practitioners still correct imbalances in the humors. They thin or thicken the blood, or administer "hot" foods when the body is too cool. A form of folk psychology, popular among evangelical Christians, characterizes individual personalities according to the four Greek "humors."

ANCIENT INDIA

Indian medical theory is similar to the Greek balance of four elements, but the Indians included a fifth: ether. According to ancient In-

Thyme was thought to be good for anemia, exhaustion, and colds. A tea made from the leaves was used as a mouthwash for mouth sores and sore throats.

Ancient physicians used mallow to treat bronchitis and stimulate the kidneys. It also made a gentle laxative and a soothing eye balm.

dian thought, the human body is made of these elements, plus it has three humors: phlegm, bile, and wind. These three are in balance in a healthy body. The Indians also assign foods different qualities. Some are hot, some are cold; and foods are given to help restore balance.

While Greek medicine was written, Indian medicine was handed down orally from genera-

Fennel is an ancient medicine used by the Chinese as an antidote for snakebite. The Greeks and Romans thought it increased strength and courage, while it prolonged youth. It was also considered to be good for the eyesight.

tion to generation. It has been established by the Indian government as the official medical practice of India, and it is taught in many universities.

ANCIENT CHINESE MEDICINE

In the early days of Chinese civilization, China was mostly Taoist, a philosophy teaching that virtue is the way to achieve health, happiness, prosperity, long life, and eventually immortality. Virtue meant living in harmony and balance with nature and avoiding extremes.

According to early Chinese philosophy, the basic elements of the universe are the forces of yin and yang. These forces are in opposition and complementary. Yin is the negative force; it is manifested in earth, damp, darkness, passivity, cold, moon, and evil. Yang is the positive force; from yang comes light, fire, beauty, activity, and good. All diseases are caused by disharmony in the forces of yin and yang. Too much yin produces chills; too much yang produces fever. Diseases caused by external forces are yang diseases; diseases coming from inside are yin diseases.

Long-ago Egyptians used the chicory plant for a tonic.

The Chinese believed that five was a fundamental number. Things occurred in groups of five; for example, there are five elements: water, fire, metal, wood, and earth. Foods are classified into five flavors: sweet, sour, pungent, bitter, and salty. These five types of food can be either "hot" or "cold" and should be eaten in balance with other hot or cold foods to maintain a proper balance in health.

As in the West at that time, Eastern physicians had no concept of infections from microscopic germs. Instead, they believed diseases came from either imbalances within the body or evil from outside. Like the Egyptians, the Chinese used a wide variety of medicines from plants, minerals, and especially animals.

Today, North Americans are sometimes revolted by the thought of medicines made from animals, especially puppies, cats, turtles, and frogs. For example, Dong Chong Xia Cao, a Chinese medicine, turns the stomachs of many Westerners. Made from a fungus that grows on the nose of certain species of caterpillars, it is a good tonic for the lungs and kidneys. The caterpillars themselves can be cooked with duck or chicken as another tonic.

The Greeks and Romans of the classical age considered verbena to be a holy herb, good for defense against demons. It also was used to treat headaches, to cleanse wounds, and as a gargle for sore throats.

Today's folk medicine is deeply rooted in ancient medical practices.

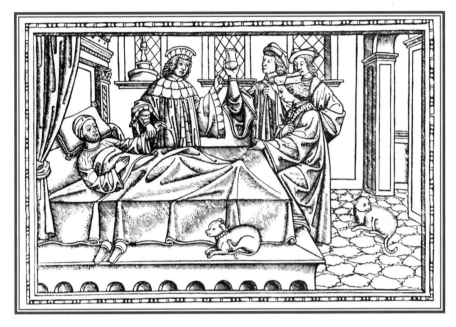

Today's folk medicine is deeply rooted in the ancient practices of China, as well as Greece, Egypt, and India. Folk practitioners may not realize that their cures come from this long-ago bedrock; instead, they simply treat people as they were taught by the healers that came before them. Without the benefit of books or "science," however, folk medicine has passed along from generation to generation, a living chain of healers that reaches thousands of years into the past.

A patient consults a folk healer.

THREE

A Different Set of Beliefs

"Science" versus "Folk"

Marigold petals (also called calendula) can be used as a stimulant and to promote perspiration. They were once thought to "comfort the heart."

WHEN YOU THINK of folk medicine, maybe you assume that it is a collection of superstitions that provide no real benefit to sick people. You might be surprised.

Many modern medical practitioners have also assumed that scientific medicine is "right" and folk medicine is "wrong." When these traditional doctors made their medicine available to a group of people, they expected it to replace "hoodoo voodoo" backwoods medicine. This didn't happen. Instead, numerous folk medicine systems function side by side with modern medicine.

People's expectations of medical care vary as widely as their backgrounds. For instance, as the scenario in chapter one indicates, a person who walks into a traditional doctor's office, may expect several things:

1. A long wait before seeing the doctor.
2. When the doctor arrives, he or she will probably be in a hurry. The patient will be expected to get right to the point.
3. Rather than listening patiently, the doctor will likely order a series of tests to make a diagnosis.
4. If the symptoms don't fit a "textbook" description of a common illness, the doctor won't want to take the extra time to research but will send the patient to another, more expensive specialist.
5. Everything in the health-care system costs vast sums of money, from the initial examination to the tests to the

specialists. (In one cartoon, a patient sits on an examining table beside her doctor as a second doctor looks into the room and says "How are you, Mrs. Jones?" The second doctor disappears in the next frame, leaving a bill for $75 for the "consultation.")

For people who aren't in the mainstream of society, who have no insurance or have limited insurance, the modern system doesn't work well. Compare this set of expectations to that of the individual who seeks treatment from a folk practitioner.

Folk medicine's traditional ingredients come directly from the Earth.

The folk medical practitioner has only a few ways to mix up and apply medicines to their patients. These are the most common ways of administering drugs.

Infusion: steeping the herb in hot water with a lid to prevent the escape of volatile oils. Water is heated up to boiling, herbs are added, covered, and allowed to cool. For example, aromatic plants such as mints are made into infusions.

Decoction: simmering over a period of time. The mixture may be left uncovered so water boils away to make the medicine stronger, unless the active principle is volatile, in which case it must remain covered. Roots and barks are often boiled into decoctions.

Poultice: grinding or pounding herbs into a moist mass that is applied to the skin for inflammations, muscle pain, or spasms. Sometimes raw plant leaves and stems are crushed and applied. Other times plants are cooked, and the liquid is thickened with flour or cornmeal.

Ointments or liniments: liquid preparation using an oil or lard as a base for external application to swollen, inflamed, or painful body parts. While the active principle may be found in the plant, the act of rubbing can also be therapeutic.

1. The folk practitioner comes to the patient's home or treats the patient from the practitioner's home.

2. Folk practitioners can only receive donations, and so they are seldom motivated by financial gain. (Neither are many traditional doctors, who must nevertheless charge large sums of money because of the huge expenses of running a modern health-care facility.)

3. Folk practitioners do not have an array of diagnostic equipment but rather depend on their own intuition and experience.

4. Folk practitioners usually come from the same area as their patients and use words the patients understand rather than medical school jargon. They listen to their patients—and listening to a patient can be as beneficial as a prescription drug.

In the case of both the folk practitioner and the trained medical doctor, the outcome is often the same: the patient usually recovers, often because the body naturally heals itself whether or  not the healer has correctly treated the illness. In one case, patients pay a lot of money, sometime feels stupid and uncomfortable, lie on a cold sterile table covered with paper, may get poked with needles, are handed a prescription, and are sent to the drug store. In the other case, patients tell the healer their troubles. They feel important, because the healer gives them her full attention. Some subjects are apt to surface in this sort of intimate conversation that wouldn't be likely to come up in a modern examination room. The healer listens, makes suggestions, and gives patients a "concoction" of some sort with directions. Patients slip a donation into the box on the way out, often feeling as though a load has been lifted from their backs.

Which patients do you think are happier with their treatment?

Modern medicine is based on the science of biology. It advances through the use of the scientific method. Double-blind tests and statistical analysis are the only way to determine how well a treatment works. Suppose, for instance, you want to determine how well chicken soup might cure the common cold. You might find approximately 1,000 people with colds. You give half of them a capsule containing chicken soup and half a "placebo," a capsule containing a useless **inert** substance.

Mint was used as an anesthetic for toothache and to promote good digestion.

Among those who received the chicken soup, perhaps 60 percent of the subjects' colds are a day shorter than the others, but only 40 percent of those who had the placebo had their cold shortened. The conclusion is that chicken soup is somewhat helpful in curing the common cold.

Now the experiment must be repeated to make sure the results are consistent. The experiment should be repeated with different quantities of chicken soup to find out what quantity is best. After spending hundreds of thousands of dollars on scientific tests, a drug company publishes its findings: "Don't buy our drugs. Just eat chicken soup for the common cold."

You can bet they won't! In order to recover their research costs, they will extract and **synthesize** the amino acids in chicken soup, patent the combination, and sell them to the doctor as a prescription medication.

Folk remedies, however, can't be patented and sold profitably by drug companies. The cost of research is too high. So the mod-

 ern doctor is limited to synthetic drugs developed by large pharmaceutical companies.

Folk practitioners use herbal remedies freely. They can't afford the cost of research and depend instead on tradition and experience for their choice of medicines. They may dig their medicines out of the swamp, the woods, or their backyard. Some form of prayer is often a part of gathering, preparing, and dispensing their medicine.

Modern medicine assumes there is no immortal spirit, or if there is, it is irrelevant to treating the body. Even psychological problems are often thought to be chemical imbalances in the brain. Most folk practitioners, however, assume a Creator made humans as a unique combination of body, soul, and spirit. This Creator takes an active interest in human beings and is willing to assist in the healing process. He gives the healer the gift of healing and directly assists the patient in healing, both through the herbs that are divinely provided for human use and through the direct and miraculous healing that comes as a result of prayer.

In modern medicine, because of the ever-increasing amount of new information, doctors tend to divide into specialties. Diseases are grouped and categorized. Patients see one specialist for one disease, another for a second problem, and perhaps a third for something else. Few doctors give thought to how each separate problem may interact with the other ones. The folk healer, however, treats the person's various conditions as part of the whole problem.

Today, folk medicine and traditional medicine are not as separated as they once were even a decade ago. Each is influenced by the other. For instance, a growing number of medical doctors are practicing "holistic medicine," a form of treatment that, like folk medicine, recognizes that an individual's various conditions are all part of one picture.

Folk medicine is not mere superstition. Instead, it is a practical and working system that for thousands of years has provided patients and practitioners with tangible benefits.

Lavender was considered to be a good cure for headaches. It was also used as a disinfectant.

FOUR

Native American Medicine

Reliance on the Earth

Native Americans used feverfew in poultices for swellings and bites. Infused in bathwater, it soothed aches and pains.

HOW NATIVE AMERICANS migrated to the Western Hemisphere is unknown. The best guess is that an accidental migration took place across the Bering Strait during an ice age, when an *isthmus* connected Asia and North America. This must have occurred 10,000 to 30,000 years ago, long before any known civilization existed to leave garbage dumps for modern archeologists to sift through.

The isolation of the two hemispheres for this period of time produced cultures and civilizations remarkably similar and different at the same time. Writing, agriculture, and metalworking appeared to arise almost simultaneously in the two hemispheres. There was perhaps more interchange between the two halves of the Earth than we will ever know.

Unknown civilizations rose and fell in North America, but by the time Europeans arrived, the population of North America consisted of a large number of small tribes with a wide variety of distinct cultures. They originally were stone-age peoples, but they quickly adopted the Europeans' horses, iron, firearms, and liquor.

Larger civilizations in southern North America and South America were more highly developed. In fact, some historians argue that Native American civilization was more advanced than Europe's of that time. The Mayans and Incas used metals, including bronze, gold, platinum, and silver. They had compulsory education and writing, and their astronomy and mathematics were comparable to that of 15th-century Europe. Complex palaces and temples displayed a high degree of engineering skill. Both

hemispheres, however, considered human life to be fairly cheap and expendable. Slavery was widespread on both sides of the Atlantic, and in the Americas human sacrifice was common.

The extent of separation between the two hemispheres meant that the Native Americans had no physical resistance to European diseases such as smallpox. When Native Americans encountered the microorganisms that caused these diseases, they died in massive numbers. Because Native Americans lived in smaller groups where the transmission of such diseases was limited, they apparently had not developed their own versions of exotic diseases to spread to Europeans.

Europeans were amazed by the health and stamina of the Native Americans. Archeologists find little evidence of osteoporosis, tooth decay, arthritis, or tuberculosis in the skeletons of these long-ago North Americans. Early Native Americans could expect to live 100 years; clearly, their lifestyle was a healthy one. (Today, however, their life span is much shorter, and European diseases still strike them proportionally harder.) Before the coming of the Europeans, the native medical practices were effective for their population.

Modern Native Americans continue to practice many of these ancient treatments in a form of folk medicine. However, lumping all Native American medicine together is a bit like combining all the medicine of Africa, Asia, and Europe into one system in order to compare and contrast it with the medicine of North and South America. North America is a big continent, and its native tribes are varied, each possessing a unique and diverse culture and customs.

Modern drugs—both illegal and prescription—are often derived from native medicines. For instance, both cocaine and Novocain come from the coca plant, which grew in southern North America and South America. Native Americans used the coca plant for pain relief.

Native Americans used balm to treat wounds.

In addition, since the coming of the Europeans to North America, the original population of North America dwindled to only a small fraction compared to what it was just before the Europeans arrived. Entire tribes were wiped out by war and diseases. The knowledge and traditions of these tribes are forever lost to the modern world.

To complicate the situation even more, over the last four to five hundred years, medical practices have so commingled between natives and Europeans that they are no longer two separate entities. The European settlers learned about their new home from the natives; they learned which North American plants were good for healing, and they benefited from many of the native medicines.

Native North Americans lived in harmony with nature, harvesting wild roots and berries and hunting wild game. For them, Earth was their mother, the source of sustenance; she gave them food, clothing, medicine, and protection. As a result, they held the Earth in solemn respect, and they studied her closely. Over thousands of years, they developed a large repertoire of plants that were good for treating a wide variety of illnesses. The tribe's medicine man

THE DOCTRINE OF SIGNATURES

The doctrine of signatures refers to the belief that when God created plants, He designed them to indicate their use by their shapes. For example, a walnut looks somewhat like a brain and therefore is useful for treating illnesses of the brain. (That is probably why people with mental illness are sometimes callously referred to as "nuts.") Plants that resemble various body parts are used for treating those body parts. The doctrine of signatures actually works in a small percentage of cases.

While the concept of the doctrine of signatures is European in origin, Native Americans also thought of plants' shapes and colors as being suggestive of their use. Many plants can be identified as "signature" plants by their name and appearance.

For instance, the name *hepatica* comes from the Latin root word for liver and refers to the three-lobed liver shape of this plant's leaf. (Hepatica is a beautiful woodland flower that blooms in the early spring. It has small white or pinkish blossoms and is found in woodlands of the United States and Canada.) Other common names include kidney liver leaf and liverwort (*wort* means "plant" in old English). Infusions of hepatica are a folk treatment for all diseases of the liver, as well as for coughs and bleeding in the lungs.

Bloodroot, *Sanguinaria canadensis*, is another spring-blooming woodland flower with a medicinal use. It has distinctively lobed leaves and a pretty white blossom; the root is finger sized and when broken, a thick red sap drips out. The root is the primary part used in medicine. Both the common and Latin names indicate the blood-like color of the sap (*sanguis* means "blood" in Latin), and Native Americans originally used the plant in the treatment of various blood diseases. European settlers quickly adopted the treatment; they also learned to use this folk medicine for a number of conditions, including chronic bronchitis, laryngitis, asthma, whooping cough and other respiratory problems, and ringworm, warts, and other skin disorders.

might be the expert in healing, but a general knowledge of what plants worked for what illnesses and where they grew was nearly universal throughout native communities.

Three hundred years ago, the medicine practiced by Native Americans did not seem particularly strange to the European settlers. In many cases, the native understanding of healing was more advanced than the European one—for instance, Native Americans knew to isolate patients with communicable diseases to prevent the spread of disease—but in general, the settlers' understanding of healing was quite similar to the native one. Like the Europeans, Native Americans used poultices from plants for cuts and sprains and to reduce swelling. Both groups also used infusions, decoctions, and ointments made from natural substances; both believed in spiritual as well as physical causes for diseases; and both depended on prayer as a form of treatment.

Native Americans' medicine differed from Europeans', however, in the ceremonial form of their prayer. Tribe members called on the spirit world to assist healing through dancing and chanting. At an early age, men who showed the proper inclination were taught the secrets, rituals, and legends used for healing. They, like the healers of other cultures, were held in high esteem and advised tribal leaders as well as practiced their art.

Ground ivy was a Native American treatment for backache and bruises. Tea made from the leaves was used to ease colds, kidney complaints, and tired eyes.

Tea made from hops was used as both a tonic and a sedative. Sleeping on pillows stuffed with the leaves was thought to calm the nerves and soothe toothache.

The tea made from elder leaves has been used for thousands of years to soothe burns, bruises, and skin conditions. Elderflower tea is said to calm the nerves, ease headaches, cool fevers, and heal throat infections. The natural painkiller found in the berries was used to treat the flu, coughs, and sore throats.

Native Americans used yellow flag to induce vomiting.

Today, both plant lore and ritual are still important parts of Native American folk medicine. For instance, many tribes build "sweat lodges" for vapor baths. Fire-heated rocks are dropped into containers of water, until the stifling moist heat induces sweating in the patient. This is thought to cleanse **toxins** from the body, but it is also a spiritual experience that brings healing and cleansing to the entire person.

Like other forms of folk medicine, Native American tradition sees no division between an individual's body and spirit. From this point of view, a healthy spirit and a healthy body are integrally linked. Native folk practices continue to offer the modern world a perspective based on centuries of knowledge and insight.

Borage was thought to promote courage and cheerfulness while it drove away sadness. Recent research indicates that it stimulates the adrenal glands. Appalachian folk healers used it to cool fevers.

FIVE

Appalachian Folk Remedies
Curative Therapies, Salt, and Kerosene

The seedpods from star anise can be used as a digestive herb. They are also a breath sweetener and can be used as a tooth cleanser.

THE APPALACHIAN MOUNTAINS range from Georgia in the south to Pennsylvania in the north. The region is often characterized as economically depressed. Folks there once made their living mining coal, working on railroads, logging, hunting, and trapping. Farmers scraped a bare living off thin rocky soil on steeply sloping fields. Poor roads restricted travel, and before the modern world-shrinking inventions such as the telephone, radio, and television, a distinct, independent culture developed.

The inhabitants kept many of their Old-World medical practices. Doctors were available but might be several hours away, and they had to be paid, so medical doctors were called in as a last resort. People relied on their own knowledge of herb lore, and for more serious cases, they usually knew a healer in the area.

The healer was a person who gathered up family folk knowledge learned from neighbors and physicians. Such a person often kept a notebook of cures and procedures. A couple of medical handbooks such as *The People's Home Medical Book,* a **lancet**, a "tooth drawer" (dental pliers), and a "clyster tube" (for enemas) might fit in his or her medical bag, along with a few store-bought patent medicines and some home-gathered herbal concoctions.

THE PROPERLY STOCKED HOME MEDICAL CHEST

One hundred years ago, an Appalachian healer would go to the store and purchase these items to have on hand. Some are still available, while some are illegal today (because of their misuse).

Appliances and Supplies
- scales for measuring scruple and dram weights
- a graduated glass container for measuring fluids
- a medicine dropper
- a hard rubber syringe
- camel's hair brushes
- absorbent cotton
- rolled bandages made from surgeon's gauze or old muslin and linen
- court plaster
- rubber adhesive
- paraffin paper

Internal Medicines
- olive oil
- glycerin
- whiskey, gin, and/or sherry wine
- magnesia
- castor oil
- syrup of rhubarb
- baking soda
- sweet spirits of nitre
- essence of peppermint and wintergreen
- syrup of ipecac

- hive syrup
- paregoric
- laudanum (made from opium)
- quinine
- soda mint
- aromatic spirits of ammonia

External Medicines

- alcohol
- ammonia water
- turpentine
- chloroform (used as an anesthetic)
- soap liniment
- extract of witch hazel
- tincture of iodine
- boric acid (an antiseptic)
- flaxseed meal
- petroleum jelly
- benzoated lard
- zinc ointment

For Poisoning

- vinegar
- tannic acid
- Epsom salts
- sulfate of copper

The local "real" doctor, if he or she has the wisdom, sees the local healer as an ally rather than competition. (Indeed, only a few generations ago, a licensed medical doctor was scarcely better trained than local healers.) Folk healers often know when they are in over their heads and will recommend the medical

Bryony is poison. Appalachian folk healers sometimes used it to relieve headache and dropsy. Most commonly, it was used to make a person vomit violently, thereby purging the body of poison.

doctor to their patients. And the wise medical doctor who is always looking for better ways to do things may pick up a few useful tricks or cures from the healer.

CURATIVE THERAPIES

Many of modern Appalachia's folk treatments are medically sound and beneficial. In the past, however, some were actually harmful.

For instance, the balancing of the humors or fluids in the body was performed excessively in the past. When a person suffered an illness that required cleansing or purifying, the healer had several choices and used them frequently and often in combination. The unfortunate patient looked forward to bleeding, sweating, blisters, purging, or vomiting. It is a tribute to the miraculous nature of the body that it could ever heal itself in spite of all manner of indignities performed upon it even when it was in a weak state. Perhaps only the strongest survived.

Bleeding
Leeches were sometimes used for bleeding a patient, but more often the healer used a lancet or good old-fashioned pocketknife.

It didn't hurt much more than the needles used today for drawing blood—unless your healer was a little shaky with the knife or didn't keep the tools sharp. A suction cup was placed over the wound to create a vacuum to draw out blood quickly and so that the healer could remove measured amounts. Bleeding was considered good for:

- pleurisy (fluid in the chest cavity resulting in painful breathing),
- sore throat,
- chest pains,
- various injuries and broken bones,
- diarrhea,
- weeping eye,
- fainting,
- vertigo (dizziness),
- spider bite,
- and many more medical conditions.

In the springtime, bleeding was performed as a preventative treatment. Members of a community were all bled at once to clear out the old, tired, and dirty blood.

If bleeding didn't help at first, it was repeated several times until the patient improved. If the patient didn't improve (or die), the healer might try another treatment, such as purging.

Purging, the Universal Cure

Taking a laxative or cathartic to "clear the bowels" is still a folk treatment in Appalachia. Milk of Magnesia or some other over-the-counter laxative may be used today, but in the past many purgatives were used, both natural and chemical, and some are still taken as a form of folk medicine. These include:

- Glauber's salts,
- cream of tartar,
- calomel,
- rhubarb,
- mayapples,
- castor oil,
- and various other mixtures.

Generally, the medicine was consumed at intervals until it had done its work, and the intestines were thoroughly cleansed.

Bleeding, purging, and blistering were not always considered to be folk treatments. In fact, at one time, these were considered to be standard medical practices—often with disastrous results.

For instance, George Washington suffered an "inflammatory infection of the upper part of the wind-pipe," perhaps what is currently called bronchitis. He hired a bleeder who removed about a pint of blood. The next day another physician removed blood twice more, plus raised blisters on his skin by applying an irritant. He also administered a purgative dose of calomel. These procedures were meant to draw bad blood away from the windpipe. Later, two more physicians came in and removed another quart of blood, still without the desired effect.

They removed two and a half quarts of blood in 13 hours—and still the great man died without a struggle. He was practically bled dry! Critics, however, complained that the doctors could have removed blood nearer the source of the problem. Open the vein under the tongue and one ounce of blood removed would be worth a quart drawn from the arm! No one questioned the use of bleeding, only the manner in which it was carried out.

If the purging didn't solve the problem, the healer could induce vomiting.

Vomiting

Emetics are medicines to cause vomiting. Ipecac is still the most commonly used emetic. Anyone who has suffered a stomach "bug" knows that sometimes clearing the stomach can greatly relieve cramps and nausea. Sometimes it doesn't help, though—and in that case, the healer may turn to sweating.

Sweating

This treatment is still used for fevers. In the past, it was thought to cure measles, hydrophobia (rabies), rheumatism, swelling, colds, bronchitis, laryngitis, pneumonia, grip (flu), and other illnesses. Sweating "equalized circulation" and "relieved congestion" of fluid in the patient.

To promote sweating, all sorts of hot beverages were used, including teas made from:

- ginger,
- boneset,
- horehound,
- elderberry blossoms,
- sage,
- slippery elm,
- and lemonade.

A popular external sweat-inducer was the "corn sweat." Here are the directions:

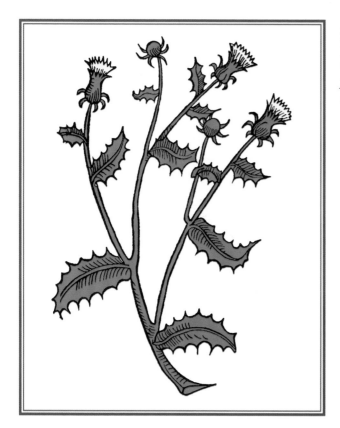

Appalachian healers used endive as a tonic and to promote the digestion. A tea made from the leaves was considered to be a good treatment for anemia and skin conditions. It was also thought to purify the blood.

Boil 20 ears of corn until a boiled corn smell is noticed. Wrap the corn in towels and place over the patient's feet, hips, arms, and neck.

This treatment was known to "break up" many diseases. (Whether or not it worked, the home-maker had dinner half prepared.) If sweating didn't clear up the trouble, however, the healer had one more option—blistering.

Tansy leaves were used in a poultice to treat sprains and aching joints.

APPALACHIAN SNAKEBITE CURE

If bitten on a limb, tie a rope or handkerchief around the limb just above the wound. Cleanse the wound at once. Suck the wound. Cut the wound open so the blood will flow freely, then fill it with salt, or if you have it, use permanganate of potash diluted three fourths with water, followed by full doses of brandy or whiskey.

After this, apply bruised plantain leaves and give a teaspoonful of the juice from the bruised leaves every hour. If plantain isn't available, kill a chicken and while warm, cut open and lay upon the wound, entrails and all, and it will draw out the poison. Or apply a poultice of onions and salt. Cauterize by applying a red-hot iron.

(If the victim survived, he was fortunate!)

Blistering

Either Spanish fly (a dried insect) or mustard seeds were prepared into a blistering plaster with tallow, beeswax, butter, and pine gum. This ointment irritated the skin, raising a blister, which was then opened and drained. The disease-causing poisons were thought to be drained from the body in this way.

By the time, patients were bled and purged, and after they had vomited, sweated, and blistered, many had gotten over their illness. If not, the healer could simply try different methods of bleeding, purging, sweating, or blistering. Eventually, the unhappy patient would surely either improve—or die.

MAKING DO

Poverty is still common in Appalachia—but the less you have available to you, the more uses you find for what you do have. For instance, every household, no matter how poor, has staples such as salt and kerosene. Salt is used both for seasoning and for the preservation of meat, while kerosene, once used for oil lamps, is still used as a heating fuel.

According to common folk traditions, the home practitioner can use common table salt for:

- *neuralgia*,
- toothache and earache (use a bag of warm salt applied like a heat pack),
- croup (1 teaspoon of salt with a teaspoon of honey),
- diarrhea and *dysentery* (dissolve salt in vinegar and warm water),
- dyspepsia and stomach troubles (use salt water),
- a *tonic*,
- a purgative, internal antiseptic,
- bath salts to beautify and strengthen the skin,
- a mouthwash to freshen breath,
- sprains and swellings (bathe freely in salt water to draw fluids out and reduce swelling),
- hair tonic,
- pin worms,
- *catarrh*,
- eye wash,
- *ague*,
- hives,

- heartburn, and
- sore throat.

Many of these treatments are safe and beneficial. You might even want to try them yourself.

Folk practice considers kerosene to be nearly as essential to the well-stocked medicine chest as salt. However, don't experiment with these old-time Appalachian treatments:

- For rheumatism, rub frequently with kerosene. (Petroleum was a favorite Native American rheumatism remedy.)
- For croup, take kerosene internally and also apply to the throat.
- For toothache, wet a piece of cotton in kerosene and insert in tooth cavity.
- For colds, every two to three hours take ten drops of kerosene on a lump of sugar. Also rub on neck and chest.
- For sore lungs, soak a cloth in kerosene and bind on the chest at night.
- For diphtheria, swab the throat with kerosene every two or three hours to remove the membrane and reduce inflammation.
- For quinsy (tonsillitis), use kerosene both internally and externally.
- For lice, apply kerosene to hair like shampoo.
- For dandruff, mix kerosene with a little glycerin to cleanse the scalp.
- For vegetable poisoning, apply externally until relief is obtained. (Next time avoid poison vegetables.)

Appalachian folk medicine is a mixture of tried-and-true treatments—and superstition. Sometimes, a particular treat-

Self-heal was a treatment for wounds.

ment becomes associated with a particular condition simply because of tradition. For instance, a person's mother may have tried kerosene as rheumatism liniment, and found that it helped her feel better (partly, perhaps, because simply rubbing the aching joint increased circulation). When she got a toothache a few months later, she decided to try kerosene for that as well—and coincidentally the pain in her tooth may have eased. From then on, she will recommend kerosene to her children as a treatment for toothache, who will in turn pass this treatment on to their own children.

If you find yourself scoffing at this basis for folk medicine, you should be aware that traditional medicine sometimes functions in the same way. Take a look at the use of antibiotics, for example.

Antibiotics help the body fight off bacteria; this means they can be useful in treating bacterial infections—but they can do nothing against viral infections (like the common cold, for instance, or the flu). Many patients (and some doctors), however, have considered antibiotics to be a sort of miracle cure, and antibiotics have been prescribed for all manner of illnesses, whether or not the condition is caused by a bacteria. Today, researchers have found that the over-use of antibiotics has actually been harmful, since resistant strains of bacteria have developed as a result.

Appalachian folk medicine cannot be dismissed as backwoods superstition. Much wisdom has been preserved and passed along by these traditions. If foolishness and superstition exist as well—well, as human beings, none of us are immune!

Wild hawthorn berries are thought to promote healing.

SIX

African American Folk Cures
Root Medicine

Root doctors use teas made from various herbs.

ROOT MEDICINE is the traditional form of medicine practiced by African Americans and some whites in the rural South, as well as in some northern urban ghetto areas. The roots of plants are frequently used for herbal cures, but root medicine also involves curing with the use of magical spells and hexes.

The origins of root medicine can be traced back to Africa and the medicine man, a health-care professional who not only treated diseases with various herbs but used magic to control evil forces. Diseases could be physical or spiritual in nature and it was often difficult to tell the difference. Healing was accomplished by trying various treatments, depending on the apparent symptoms.

When blacks came to America as slaves, they did not have access to good health care and had to make do with what they had. Even in the present, modern medical care has been expensive or difficult to obtain for many rural African Americans. They have been forced to rely on other methods of dealing with sickness. Early African Americans learned some medical concepts from slave owners, such as the humor classifications of disease. Some of the plant lore of the Native Americans was also adopted.

As African Americans converted to Christianity, the role of the medicine man changed. Magic was now often thought to be the work of the devil. Wicked people used spells and hexes, while the church handled healing or the removal of a spell. In reality, however, both good and evil folk used a somewhat "magical" worldview.

In root medicine, diagnosing a sickness usually starts with

Nettle may be used by root doctors as a scalp tonic, to encourage hair growth and cure dandruff. The leaves contain Vitamins A and C. They can be crushed to make a stimulating rub for rheumatism. Taken internally, they act as a laxative.

assuming a natural cause rather than a supernatural cause, perhaps an imbalance in the body. The life of a person is in the blood, so a body out of balance often suffers from an imbalance in the blood. It may be too sweet or bitter, high or low, thick or thin. It may need cleansing if it has impurities in it. Blood out of balance leads to a host of symptoms in the head, stomach, lungs, or kidneys. The symptoms are treated with one of a variety of herbal concoctions.

Many older African Americans have a small number of tried-and-true herbal remedies for various sicknesses. These are the medicines of first resort. If none of these work, the person may try conventional medicine. The doctor's medicine is considered more powerful than herbal medicines but more dangerous and less natural.

An illness that fails to respond either to herbal cures or professional medical treatment is considered to be a mental problem, either a punishment sent by God for an unrepented sin or an illness caused by a spell or hex placed on the person by someone who wishes harm to the individual. If the problem is traced to sin, the person seeks the help of a faith healer or church leader. Healing is achieved through confession, repentance, and restoration in the church.

If the situation seems to be caused by an evil spell, the person may choose a root doctor. This person became a healer not through a medical education but as a calling from God. She may have received a sign that led to her calling—or her birth may have been accompanied by strange omens that told the community right from the start that this was a special person. Healing ability is considered a spiritual gift, and as the Lord's servants, root doctors practice without consideration of payment. Healers use a wide variety of methods for healing, including herbs, "magic potions," and prayer.

If a person suffers from burning pains or strange itching and rashes that don't respond to normal treatment, the cause may be a spell cast by an evil practitioner; the practitioner will have been hired by an enemy who wishes the victim harm. The problem may be animals under the skin. In this case, the witch or sorcerer made powder from the eggs of toads, lizards, or snakes and hid it in the victim's food. The animal then grows under the person's skin, causing the symptoms.

Serious chronic stomach troubles accompanied by nausea or vomiting are also believed to be the work of magical poisoning. Another condition caused by black magic is "fading," a strange kind of paralysis that starts with numbness in the arms and legs. It spreads over the body until the person can hardly walk and includes hallucinations, strange uncharacteristic behaviors, and hearing voices.

Evidence of a spell is sometimes found: a doll or mud image, bags containing the nail clippings or the hair of the victim. Often the sickness occurs after the charm is discovered, but charms don't necessarily have to be found

In *Doctors and Root Doctors: People Who Use Both*, Holly Matthews includes this case history:

A young woman develops a "bug" of some kind. She goes to work but comes home early, because she is feeling so sick. Her mother feeds her some tea to ease stomach pains. The next day she goes to the doctor, who tells her she has the flu; he gives her some pills and recommends rest and plenty of fluids.

A week later she is feeling better, but on the way home from work, she notices her old boyfriend standing on the curb with another girl. Immediately, she feels sick and barely makes it home before she begins to vomit. She and her mother discuss the last time she was sick, and the young woman remembers that shortly before she got sick, she saw the new girlfriend staring at her. Maybe that girl is jealous of her, she reasons.

The young woman goes to see her ex-boyfriend's mother, who says she doesn't like the new girlfriend. The older woman tells the young woman to go see a root doctor.

The young woman pays a visit to the root doctor, an elderly man who has lived in the community all his life. He starts by asking her what she thinks is wrong. She tells him not only about her symptoms but about her financial problems and her relationship with her old boyfriend. After an hour of talking, the root doctor diagnoses her problem: she has been bewitched by the new girlfriend's evil thoughts. He gives the young woman a potion for the present spell and some powder to sprinkle in her shoes to prevent other possible evil charms. He also advises her not to be so concerned about her old boyfriend and to think about dating other men. He suggests she come back to buy potions from him as needed.

The young woman goes home feeling a sense of peace and relief. Her physical symptoms disappear.

for a victim to suspect he has been hexed. He may have a guilty conscience and as a result he suspects that someone he has wronged may have worked a curse on him. Whether merely the suggestion of a hex or a guilty conscience  may bring on the illness is impossible to say. The person may seek help from a traditional physician, but if he does not improve, he assumes his condition is something modern medicine can't help. Time to consult the root doctor.

As practiced today, root medicine still assumes the causes of disease can be physical, spiritual, or a combination of both. Natural causes result from imbalances in the body. Often these are the result of a failure to maintain a proper balance. Overeating causes obesity, for instance, and eating an improper balance of foods can cause a variety of problems. Maintaining a healthy body requires moderation in all things. While some presuppositions of root medicine may be incorrect, this logical approach to illness yields a surprisingly effective system.

Curanderos may use yarrow to restore the appetite and promote perspiration. It is considered to be a plant of great power. The ancient Chinese used it to foretell the future.

SEVEN

Hispanic Folk Healers
Curanderos

Foxglove was once used by folk healers as a treatment for swellings and dropsy. Modern doctors discovered it contains digitalis, a powerful heart medicine.

THE FIRST EUROPEAN immigrants to the New World were the Spanish, who conquered and subjugated American Indian civilizations in South and Central America. They came looking for gold and they came to spread Christianity; the conquerors came to enslave the inhabitants, the missionaries to save and educate them.

They brought their own medical knowledge with them. As Spanish settlers intermarried with the Native Americans, medical techniques likewise intermingled. The descendants of the Aztecs and the Spanish created a new ethnic group: the Mexicans.

In the mid-1800s, the United States annexed the Southwest. Many thousands of Mexicans became American citizens. As prosperity in the north increased, Mexicans migrated to the United States, mostly as low-paid agricultural and railroad workers and miners.

Today the migration continues, both legal and illegal. Among farmers and orchard owners, Hispanic migrant workers have a reputation for an excellent work ethic with strong family values. Successful workers establish rapport with their employer, then recommend their brothers, sisters, and cousins as more employees are required. These workers do not have easy access to health care. However, they bring their folk medical knowledge with them.

Curandismo is the system of folk healing used by many Mexican Americans. The *curandero*, or healer, is a person who practices more or less full time. He or she is a person from the community and unlike a doctor is easily accessible to the people of

Parsley is rich in Vitamins A, B, and C, as well as iron and calcium. Used as a tonic, it stimulates the digestive system and kidneys. It can also be used to make an antiseptic for cuts and insect bites.

the community. Curanderos' offices are usually in their homes. No appointments are necessary, and payment is voluntary, according to the patient's conscience.

Curanderos share many characteristics with folk healers of other groups. They see their ability to heal as a gift from God. Most are Christians, and their attitude toward their gift is one of reverent thankfulness. Prayer is a major component of their healing.

Unlike modern medicine but like other folk systems, curanderos see human health as a duality of the physical and spiritual or natural and supernatural. There must be a harmonious relationship between the two parts if the body is to be healthy. Natural illnesses can best be treated with herbal remedies or by standard medical methods. Supernatural illness, however, cannot be effectively treated by modern medicine. Many illnesses can be of either natural or supernatural origin, including diabetes, alcoholism, or any other disease. These supernatural conditions might be caused by *espiritus malos* (evil spirits) or *brujos* (witches or sorcerers). Natural illnesses are best handled by either the medical profession or nonprofessional healers, leaving the more difficult cases for the curanderos.

The modern practice of curandismo has evolved out of several roots. While not all curanderos are religious, there is overall

a strong influence from Judeo-Christian religious beliefs and the practices and rituals of the Roman Catholic tradition. This religious influence is based on the many references to healing in the Old and New Testaments of the Bible. Curanderos often look to the New Testament, especially the Gospel written by Luke, a physician; they take inspiration from stories of Christ, who spent a large portion of his ministry healing the sick. According to curanderos' belief, healing comes directly from God through miracles or through the intercession of a person with the gift of healing. They base this belief on the scripture that says "to each is given the manifestation of the Spirit for the common good. To one is given through the Spirit the utterance of wisdom . . . to another gifts of healing by the one Spirit. . ." (1 Corinthians 11:7–9). Illnesses are attributed to natural causes resulting from the "fallen" state of the world, unresolved sin, or direct demonic possession. Each cause requires a different type of treatment.

Ancient Arabic medicine, which can be traced back through Greek humor traditions, had a strong influence on curandismo. The Moors introduced their system when they conquered Spain in the eighth century. According to their way of thinking, sickness and health were determined by harmony and balance in a person's humors. An ill person needed the balance restored. Curanderos still strive for this equilibrium between disease and health.

Medieval witchcraft and spiritualism have also influenced curandismo, which expects psychic phenomena to be commonplace. The

When Spanish missionaries came into contact with the Native Americans, knowledge transferred in both directions. The Spanish taught their healing methods to the natives, while the natives taught the Spanish their medicinal uses for vast numbers of herbs and plants. The plants of the New World were for the most part different than the Old World's, and the Spanish conquerors were dependent on their victims for knowledge.

Rue may be used as a disinfectant. Ancient healers from Spain considered it to be a cure for insanity.

healer is thought to harness spiritual powers through rituals, incantations, crucifixes, candles, and the Bible; each is used in specific ways for specific cures. From this perspective, the supernatural power has no will of its own but rather is controlled by the "healer." The modern curandero may accept or reject the idea of harnessing "spirit beings" to either heal or harm others. This area divides the healer from the "brujo" or sorcerer.

Researchers looking to learn about curandismo found that when interviewing curanderos, the healers performed tests on the researchers, seeking others with a healing gift. One test involved the researchers sitting in a semicircle with palms opened upward and eyes closed. The curandero prayed and told the members of the group to concentrate on God and sit in this fashion for about 15 minutes. Afterward, the group described their sensations, and the curandero perceived that one of the researchers had the healing gift. Over the course of interviewing various healers and receiving various tests, several researchers were invited to study with the healers.

Today these folk healers freely adapt anything that works from other sources, including modern science. For example, curanderos use standard terms for diseases and accept diagnoses from conventional Western medicine. They prescribe drugstore over-the-counter medicines as freely as ancient herbal remedies. If conventional medicine is more effective for a particular condition, they will refer their patients to a doctor.

In other words, curandismo is not a rigid and unchanging system. Instead, it is a living folk tradition, one that it constantly evolving to meet the needs of its community.

Acupuncture is an ancient Chinese medical technique.

EIGHT

Asian American Folk Medicine

Organs, Meridians, and Acupuncture

Many Westerners may seek out an Asian folk healer.

ASIAN FOLK MEDICINE varies from region to region. One of the most influential forms is rooted in the traditional medical practices of China. This ancient body of knowledge is quite different from Western perspectives on the human body.

Without any knowledge of internal anatomy, ancient Asian practitioners had to rely on external observation. They believed the human body contained five solid "Zang" organs: the heart, spleen, lungs, kidneys, and liver. Their conclusions, however, don't correspond with the functions of the organs as we know them. From their perspective, not only do the organs have physical attributes, but they also are believed to have psychological effects.

1. The heart controls mental activities and blood circulation. Its effects can be seen in the complexion and it is linked to the tongue. It controls all life processes.
2. The spleen controls digestion as well as the limbs and the flesh. It is linked to the lips. It stores a person's intentions and determination.
3. The lungs control respiration and maintain the downward flow of fluid. They store a person's vitality. The lungs are linked to the nose.
4. The kidneys regulate water in the body, store the "vital essence" of life, and produce bone marrow (the same material as the brain and spinal cord). The kidney's health is reflected in the hair.

5. The liver stores blood. The soul resides in the liver. The liver is linked to the eyes, and its condition can be diagnosed through the nails.

The body also contains the five "Fu" organs. These are hollow organs that correspond to one of the five solid organs.

1. The small intestine is paired with the heart. It processes water and food, converting them into useful "clear" substances. Waste or "turbid" products are excreted.
2. The stomach, a reservoir for food and water, is paired with the spleen.
3. The large intestine, paired with the lungs, concentrates solid wastes and absorbs water.
4. The urinary bladder, paired with the kidney, stores and discharges urine, separating the clear fluid from the turbid.
5. The gall bladder, paired with the liver, is a reservoir for bile, a product of the liver.

Asian medicine also believed that there were organs of consciousness: the brain, bone marrow, blood vessels, uterus, and meridians (channels running through the body and distributing "Qi" or vital energy) are all associated with consciousness or mental functioning.

Asian medicine uses various herbs.

Dried herbs may be packaged and labeled for dispensing.

MERIDIANS

A unique concept in Chinese folk medicine is the concept of meridians, channels that distribute the life force or "Qi" throughout the body. This network connects the ten organs. When the free flow of Qi is interrupted, poor health is the result. These channels can be opened through acupuncture (the insertion of needles). Each channel has different numbers of points, places where the Qi comes to the body surface. Medical treatments are performed at these sites, either acupuncture, pressure such as massage, or the application of heat.

ACUPUNCTURE

The practice of acupuncture dates back at least 4,000 years. The early needles were made from flint. Those needles were replaced with bone and bamboo and later gold and silver. Modern acupuncturists use stainless steel.

Originally, acupuncture was used mostly for lancing boils and drawing fluid from swollen or infected areas. Eventually, the Chinese learned that inserting needles in certain areas could relieve pain in other areas. Between 1000 and 200 BC, the main meridian points were located. The purpose of acupuncture shifted from simple pain relief to a way to rebalance the flow of Qi (or energy).

When European medical practices were introduced in China in the 1800s, the practice of acupuncture gradually fell into disuse and was eventually dropped from the official medical education as "backward." By the early 1900s, it was banned. Then in the mid-20th century, the communist government encouraged a revival of traditional Chinese folk practices, and a modern scientific basis for acupuncture developed. The practice eventually spread to the West. It is no longer merely a folk treatment and is used as an alternative therapy for a wide range of conditions.

Asian folk medicine is in many ways similar to Western folk medicine. Herbal remedies have been handed down from generation to generation, and the folk practitioner sees the person as a physical-spiritual creature. Illnesses are caused by imbalances of substances from within or without the body. For health to be restored, balance must be achieved.

Today Asian folk medicine is gaining popu-

Acupuncture has come to be a respected medical treatment even in the Western world.

Tai chi is a form of exercise based on the Chinese belief in "Qi." It is designed to stimulate the flow of the body's vital energy.

larity in the West as an alternative medicine. Many Westerners, including medical doctors, respect the centuries-old wisdom that can be found in this folk tradition.

THE YIN YANG DIET

While the Western medical community looks at food choices in terms of a balance of vitamins and minerals, fats and carbohydrates, Chinese folk practitioners look at the balance of yin and yang. Yang foods are considered "hot" and "dry," good for eating when the weather is cool and damp or if a person's body tends to be "yinish." Yin foods are considered "cool" and "moist," good for hot weather. Too much yin or yang, whether in food, climate, or the tendency of the body, and illness will result.

Yang foods include black tea, onions, chicken, peppers, and lamb. For proper balance, these should be served with yin foods: beans, bananas, crab, duck, and lettuce. Other foods are considered neutral: apricots, beef, eggs, corn, potatoes, pumpkin, and white rice. These can be served with yin and yang foods without changing their properties.

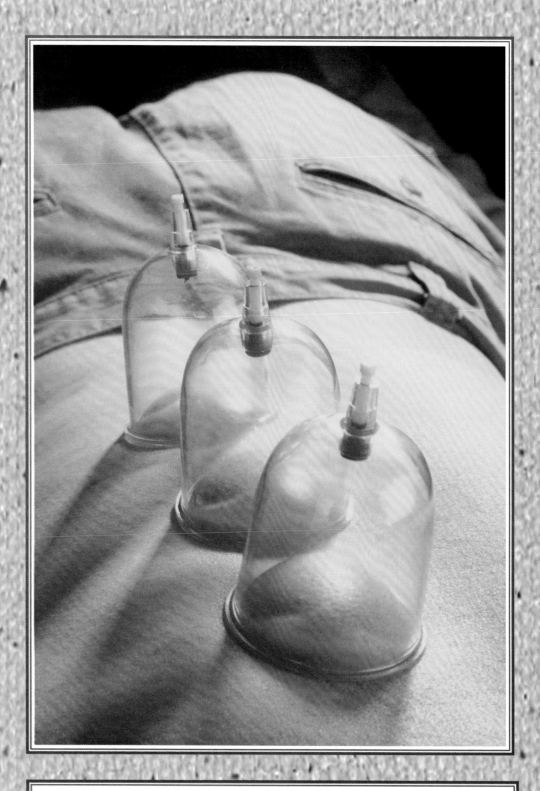

Cupping is an ancient therapy that draws blood to the surface of the skin. It has regained popularity as a modern folk treatment.

NINE

Folk Medicine Today
A Living Tradition

Aromatherapy is a folk treatment that uses the power of scent to adjust the body's equilibrium.

MOST NORTH AMERICAN children today are virtually assured of living a long healthy life. Only a hundred years ago, however, a large percentage of children could be expected to either die from disease or suffer the lifetime effects of some disease. Diseases once caused blindness, deafness, and paralysis in millions of children. Modern medicine has been very successful in treating and curing a wide variety of diseases. Conventional medicine has been one of the greatest advances of civilization.

Modern medicine has also come under a great deal of criticism. Medical care is expensive; doctors can't heal everything; and large clinics can be impersonal. As a result, many people turn back to traditional folk practices as an alternative to modern health care. Maybe, however, the complainers have forgotten or never knew what life was like even 60 years ago when polio swept through areas of the country. Today, thanks to conventional medicine, we take for granted our safety from many diseases.

But even with the huge advances in modern medicine, folk healing is not disappearing. The many forms of folk medicine are vigorous and thriving. Often, the modern clinic simply provides one more option to try.

Surveys show that the users of folk practitioners are not just uneducated and ignorant poor people who can't access modern care. Neither are they all older people from a different era or immigrants looking for care like they received in the "old country." Instead, today's users of folk medicine are often college-educated, professional people. Many will try a local healer first and save a

Marjoram is an ancient antidote for poison. It was also used to treat colds, calm the nerves, and settle the stomach. Pillows made from the leaves were thought to be good for insomnia.

doctor's visit for the last resort. These modern believers will treat mild illnesses themselves, using "natural medicines" that include beehive products, herbs from the health store, and plants they find in their own backyards.

PRODUCTS OF THE BEEHIVE

Beehive products are growing in popularity as a folk treatment. Since the beginning of civilization, honeybees have provided food and medicine for cultures in Africa, Asia, and Europe. Because of bees' importance to human health and well-being, bees were one of the first livestock imported to the New World.

Honey has been used extensively since ancient times as a medicine. Modern science has in many instances reinforced its use in folk medicine. For instance, researchers have found that honey is antibacterial; microorganisms cannot live in honey for two reasons: First, the concentration of sugar is so high that the moisture in single-celled bacteria is sucked out, and the bacteria die of thirst. Second, even when honey absorbs water and no longer dries out microorganisms, a complex chemical change occurs, and hydrogen peroxide, a powerful antibiotic, forms.

Honey is still used both internally and externally. When applied to wounds, ulcers, and burns, honey kills germs and reduces swelling in damaged tissue. Internally, honey soothes sore throats and coughs. Because honey contains minute quantities of pollen, people eat it to reduce the effect of pollen allergies. Honey is most effective that is produced by the bees at the same time a person's hay fever occurs; it apparently acts as an **immunizing** agent. People also chew beeswax to reduce allergies in the belief that the small amount of pollen in the wax allows the body to build up immunity to the pollen.

Other beehive products besides honey make good medicines as well:

- Propolis is gum gathered by the bees from various tree buds. Bees use it to seal holes and cracks in their hive; humans have found that it is also antibacterial and makes a good dressing for wounds.
- Honeybees gather pollen to feed their brood; some beekeepers collect a portion of pollen for use in medicine for the treatment of allergies.
- Bee venom is used to treat inflammatory conditions such as rheumatoid arthritis. It is also used to treat muscular dystrophy. You might wonder why people would willingly force a bee to sting them, but in fact, honeybee stings are not as painful as other stinging insects.

Monkshood is a poison. Some folk practitioners use small quantities as a sedative or a painkiller.

MEDICINES IN THE BACKYARD

Watch out! You may be stepping on a medicinal plant right now. Medicinal plants are everywhere. You can find these plants right in your yard, along the roadside, or in a nearby hedge.

Dandelion

This "weed" was once used as a "spring tonic." Back when people couldn't get fresh vegetables in the winter, they often suffered from malnourishment. Dandelion was one of the first greens they could harvest in the spring. It is full of vitamins A, B, and C, so it really is good for you. It was used to treat liver, gall bladder, and spleen problems, as well as urinary tract complaints. It is mild, wholesome, and safe. It is also quite bitter, so it should be eaten while it is very young.

Plantain

Often called "medicine plant," it is found from coast to coast across North America. It is also known as soldier's herb, plantago, and by several dozen other names. It grows in yards, vacant lots, on the shoulder of the road, and in other waste places. Some people consider it a noxious weed, and it is a bane to people with an allergy to its pollen, but plantain seeds have been used as a laxative and for treating **dropsy** and **jaundice**. The crushed leaves are used on

The bruised leaves of the plantain are good for insect bites, stings, wounds, and burns.

FOLK CURE STOPS BLEEDING

Evan looked down and gasped. A huge leech had attached itself to his leg. Of course it hadn't been huge when it first found Evan wading through the muddy creek. The leech had sucked his blood, first injecting its saliva, which contained an enzyme to prevent the blood from clotting. Slowly, it gorged itself on Evan's blood, until it was swollen into a blue-black pulsing glob.

Evan's dad immediately removed the leech and killed it. The wound continued to bleed slowly, soaking bandage after bandage. It bled for hours. Evan's parents leafed through old medical books and found that puffball spores will staunch bleeding—but summer is not a good time to find puffballs. They also found that plantain or "medicine plant" was once used on wounds. They crushed a leaf into a damp pulp and bandaged it to the leg. Within minutes, the bleeding stopped.

cuts and abrasions to soothe the skin and stop bleeding. The leaves can be bruised and wrapped around a cut, then tied with string for a primitive bandage. When boiled, the leaves were once used to cure gout (excess of uric acid in tissues resulting in swelling and severe pain).

Sumac

This common shrub has a bad reputation because of its cousin the poison sumac. Poison sumac has whitish berries, however, while the beneficial staghorn sumac has bright red berries clustered in a shape like an upside down cone. The berries can be used for "Indian lemonade" by scraping them off the stem into a container. Add approximately twice the volume of water, stir, and strain out the berries. This sour drink can be used as a lemon

Rosemary makes a good skin rinse. It was once thought to be a preserver of youth and was burned as a protection against infection. It also makes a good natural dandruff treatment. The first printed English herbal contained these directions for the use of rosemary: "Boil the leaves in white wine and wash thy face therewith . . . thou shalt have a fair face . . . wash thyself and thou shalt wax shiny."

or vinegar substitute. Add sugar to taste for pink lemonade. The unsweetened "tea" can also be applied to wounds to stop bleeding or used on burns or infections. It soothes skin diseases such as eczema, shingles, or ringworm. Taken internally, it helps dysentery and sore throats. When the berries are out of season, a tea can be made from the bark and roots for treating the same conditions as the berries.

Coltsfoot

One of the earliest of spring wildflowers, coltsfoot often grows along roadsides where little else grows. The flowers resemble small dandelions, and the leaves, which arrive after the flowers are gone, are the size and shape of a colt's hoof. It was once used as a remedy for coughs, bronchitis, and asthma. The leaves

Chiropractors were once considered to be folk practitioners. Today, however, they have gained the respect of the traditional medical community.

were dried and smoked—the cure may have been worse than the illness! Native Americans and early settlers also made a tea by boiling the dried leaves in water for half an hour. Cloth soaked in the tea was laid over the throat or chest to relieve symptoms.

Burdock

Boiled young roots, usually a teaspoon of chopped roots to a cup of water, were used as a wash for skin ailments and diseases,

TANNIC ACID, THE "MIRACLE DRUG"

If you were marooned on a desert island and could pick one drug to take with you, what would you choose? Aspirin, acetaminophen, ibuprofen? You probably wouldn't choose tannic acid. That should, however, be the first medicine you looked for on the island, because it is such a common ingredient in plants, and it is perhaps the most useful of the commonly occurring natural medicines.

Tannic acid is used to tan hides, from which it derives its name. But tannic acid is also a natural disinfectant. Plants and trees high in tannic acid content resist decay.

Tannic acid is an astringent (it shrinks tissue), which means it helps the body to heal bleeding internally as well as externally. It can be used in a beverage to soothe sore or scratchy throats and coughs. It also is used for dysentery, diarrhea, and diseases of kidney, bladder, and urethra.

Tannic acid is water-soluble and is available simply by boiling plants containing it. Black tea, for instance, contains tannic acid. One of the most common folk remedies for a sore throat is to make a strong tea with lemon, lightly sweetened with honey. Tannic acid is also found in sumac berries, acorns, oak galls, and blackberry leaves, roots, and seeds. An effective antidiarrheal beverage can be made by boiling blackberries and sweetening until it's palatable.

Many folk techniques and drugs find their way into conventional medicine. Scientists perform double-blind tests and discover many folk remedies really work. Nevertheless, some folk medicine recipes seem wildly absurd. Imagine taking a dose of "Shiloh's Consumption Cure" (used for colds, coughs, bronchitis, asthma, and irritation of the throat). Here are the ingredients:

muriatic acid (available at the uto supply store)
muriate of morphine
extract of ginger
extract of wild cherry
extract of henbane
dilute alcohol
chloroform
essence of peppermint
syrup of tar

No wonder the average life span a hundred years ago was about 45 years!

burns, wounds, and scalds. The resulting bitter tea could also be used internally as a tonic and for rheumatism.

Heal All

The name pretty much says it. Once you identify this plant, you can clean out the medicine cabinet! According to folk medicine belief, you won't need anything else.

Mustard

Now a common weed, this is the same plant used to make the bright yellow mustard you put on your hot dog. Coarse leaves

An infusion of pennyroyal leaves is good for coughs, hoarseness, and indigestion.

Aromatherapy can be used to calm and soothe the nerves.

Purslane leaves cool inflamed eyes. A tea made from purslane reduces fevers.

and bright yellow flowers make it easy to identify. The leaves should be dampened with cold water and placed on painful body parts for its pain-relieving effects. Poultices and plasters are made from mustard, vinegar, breadcrumbs, and egg whites. When applied to the skin, the blood vessels dilate, increasing circulation. Left on too long, however, mustard plasters can cause blisters. The poultices were used for treating headaches and neuralgia. Adding

The roots of the blackberry plant may be used to treat diarrhea.

ground mustard seeds to drinking water produces an emetic (induces vomiting). Honey mixed with mustard was sometimes used as cough medicine.

THESE are just a few of the folk medicines available today. In the 21st century, more medical alternatives are available than at any other time in history. North American's big "melting pot" has mixed up a wide variety of healing traditions from all over the globe. As a result, people can benefit from conventional medicine—and at the same time choose to supplement their health care with folk medicine. When science and folk traditions combine, people benefit from centuries of accumulated wisdom from around the world.

Further Reading

Hatfield, Gabrielle. *Memory, Wisdom, and Healing: The History of Domestic Plant Medicine.* New York: Sutton, 2000.

Jarvis, D.C. *Folk Medicine.* New York: Fawcett Crest, 1991.

Moss, Kay K. *Southern Folk Medicine.* Colombia: University of South Caroline, 1999.

Root-Bernstein, Robert. *Honey, Mud, Maggots, and Other Medical Marvels: The Science Behind Folk Remedies.* New York: Houghton Mifflin, 1998.

Trotter, Robert T. II. *Curanderismo: Mexican American Folk Healing.* Athens: University of Georgia Press, 2000.

Wilen, Joan and Lydia Wilen. *Chicken Soup and Other Folk Remedies.* New York: Ballantine, 2000.

For More Information

Cultural Diversity and Folk Medicine
www.temple.edu

General Folk Medicine
www.folkmedicine.net
www.folkzone.com/FolkMedicine

Hispanic Folk Medicine
riceinfo.rice.edu

UCLA Folk Medicine Database
www.folkmed.ucla.edu

Glossary

Ague Shivering fits or chills.

Catarrh Nasal inflammation.

Dropsy Medical condition where water is retained in body tissues.

Dysentery Severe diarrhea.

Immunizing Producing antigens against a specific infection.

Inanimate Nonliving.

Inert Unmoving.

Isthmus A narrow connecting strip of land.

Jaundice A condition where the skin turns yellow due to improper functioning of the liver.

Lancet A sharp, pointed surgical instrument.

Medieval Having to do with the Middle Ages, the period of European history from about AD 500 to 1500.

Neuralgia Pain along a nerve.

Papyri Scrolls made from the pith of the papyrus plant.

Synthesize Create artificially.

Tonic A substance that increases or restores physical and emotional tone.

Toxic Poison.

Index

Biographies

Peter Sieling is the owner of Garreson Lumber and the author and publisher of two technical books: *Bee Hive Construction* and *Air Drying Lumber for Maximum Yield*. In addition, he writes for *Bee Culture Magazine*. He enjoys playing the keyboard, harmonica, and banjo. He resides with his wife and three children in upstate New York, where several pea fowls, a goose, approximately 500,000 honeybees, and assorted cats and dogs also keep him company.

Dr. Alan Jabbour is a folklorist who served as the founding director of the American Folklife Center at the Library of Congress from 1976 to 1999. Previously, he began the grant-giving program in folk arts at the National Endowment for the Arts (1974–76). A native of Jacksonville, Florida, he was trained at the University of Miami (B.A.) and Duke University (M.A., Ph.D.). A violinist from childhood on, he documented old-time fiddling in the Upper South in the 1960s and 1970s. A specialist in instrumental folk music, he is known as a fiddler himself, an art he acquired directly from elderly fiddlers in North Carolina, Virginia, and West Virginia. He has taught folklore and folk music at UCLA and the University of Maryland and has published widely in the field.